D0427268

DISCARD

More Advance Praise for

THE ART OF INFLUENCE

"To have SUCCESS, you need to be a person of influence. Mastering *The Art of Influence* will help you inspire your family, your colleagues, and your community to their own greater potential . . . Take your influence to another level by reading this great little book today!"

—Darren Hardy, publisher, *Success* magazine

"Chris has powerfully influenced thousands of individuals and organizations. Now, with *The Art of Influence*, it's *your* turn!"

—Denis Waitley, author of *Seeds of Greatness*

"Another winner! Concise, easy to read, and full of valuable takeaways."

—John P. Strelecky, international bestselling author of *The Why Café*

"*The Art of Influence*, Chris Widener's newest work, once again displays his ability to wrap a charming tale around an important lesson: character matters more than skill. I highly recommend this book to business people who are on a quest for continual personal and professional growth."

—Laura Stack, MBA, CSP, author of *Leave the Office Earlier*

"Contrary to popular thinking, it's not talent, education, or intelligence that's primarily responsible for success—it is influence. No one knows this, or teaches this, better than Chris Widener . . . A simple yet fascinating and powerful story that you'll want to share with everyone in your organization."

—Vic Johnson, founder, AsAManThinketh.net

"We learn best through experiences . . . ours and those of others. The artfully woven story in this book will have you feeling as if YOU are the one having this experience. And you will learn . . . a lot! . . . You'll be a better person for having read this book."

—Jim Cathcart, author of *The Acorn Principle*

"The sooner you take Chris Widener's four golden rules of influence and apply them to your life, the sooner you will be on your way to success! After all, nothing is better than GOLD!"

–April Humphrey, executive V.P.,
International Leadership Development Inc.

"Chris has taken some extremely well-thought-out concepts and turned them into a story that you can't put down. The messages are very powerful and life-changing if applied. This is not only a must-read for anyone in business, but for anyone seeking a richer life."

—Brad Worthley, CEO, Brad Worthley International

"*The Art of Influence* is a magnificent teaching on how to be successful and influential. It cuts through complicated technique and takes you right to the four rules that—if you'll live by them—will forever make you rich; both in business and in life."

—Bob Burg, author of *Endless Referrals* and coauthor of *The Go-Giver*

"Chris Widener has struck 'gold' again! Through simple, yet powerful storytelling, you will come to know the Four Golden Rules of Influence that will change forever how you attain long-lasting success and happiness. Become the individual others want to follow by reading this extraordinary tale."

—Colette Carlson, founder, SpeakYourTruth.com

"Chris Widener's *The Art of Influence* is an entertaining, thought-provoking, and fun guide to one of the most practical skills that will lead you to personal success. Chris has a well-earned reputation of being a master at teaching you to turn your potential into your full potential."

—Patricia Fripp, CSP, CPAE,
past president, National Speakers Association,
author of *Make It, So You Don't Have to Fake It!*

"*The Art of Influence* is as good as 'gold'! A short, delightful read that is long on valuable and practical leadership principles. I loved it and highly recommend it!"

—Tom Flick, Tom Flick Communications
and Outlook Consulting Group

"Chris Widener understands the true essence of success and life. *The Art of Influence* is a powerful book that gives us all important insight about what really matters. This book will touch your heart, make you think, and influence you in a positive way."

—Mike Robbins, CSP, author of
Focus on the Good Stuff: The Power of Appreciation

"Chris Widener's principle-based stories have had a tremendous impact on our organization. His newest book is a must for any personal-growth library."

—Ryan D. Chamberlin,
National Companies, Double-Platinum, Presidential Director

THE ART OF INFLUENCE

The

ART

of

INFLUENCE

Persuading Others Begins with You

CHRIS WIDENER

DOUBLEDAY

New York   London   Toronto   Sydney   Auckland

DD
DOUBLEDAY

Copyright © 2008 by Chris Widener

All Rights Reserved

Published in the United States by Doubleday,
an imprint of The Doubleday Publishing Group,
a division of Random House, Inc., New York.
www.doubleday.com

DOUBLEDAY is a registered trademark
and the DD colophon is a trademark of Random House, Inc.

All trademarks are the property of their respective companies.

Book design by Jennifer Ann Daddio

Cataloging-in-Publication Data is on file
with the Library of Congress.

ISBN 978-0-385-52103-1

PRINTED IN THE UNITED STATES OF AMERICA

1   3   5   7   9   10   8   6   4   2

First Edition

The Art of Influence
is dedicated to men and women everywhere
striving to be influencers who lead their
families, businesses, communities, and
countries to greater heights.

THE ART OF INFLUENCE

GRANDMA'S GIFT

It was a perfect Sunday summer afternoon for a barbecue to honor a young man who had worked so hard to achieve his dreams. The sun was shining and the temperature hovered around seventy-five degrees. Friends and family were gathered together, some of whom had not seen each other for years. Kids played in and around the swimming pool and the smell of burgers wafted through the backyard. Perfect.

Marcus Drake had a lot to be thankful for. His parents, Bill and Margaret Drake, were classic middle-class, middle-America folks who'd worked hard to give their children a good life. Bill was an insurance salesman and Margaret had been a homemaker, staying home to take care of Marcus and his brother, Jack, who was two years younger. Margaret was part cook, part cleaning lady, part nurse, and part taxi driver to the two boys who were the love of her life. Bill was there for most of the boys' games and school events and did his best to get home for dinner with Margaret and the boys every night. The Drakes had the classic *Ozzie and Harriet* existence.

The barbecue was to celebrate Marcus's graduation from Northwestern's Kellogg School of Management and everyone was thrilled to be there. Few of the Drakes had gone to college, let alone business school. No, the Drakes were a simple family.

Marcus, however, wanted a different kind of life. He always had, in fact. In high school Marcus had been a three-sport athlete, lettering in football, basketball, and baseball, and had usually made all-league. But he wasn't good enough to get a full ride to a major college, so he decided to focus on school rather than sports in college.

Marcus grew up watching TV shows that showed the lifestyles of business moguls and for as long as he could remember had wanted to become one himself. He had read *Forbes* and *Fortune* since his early teens. He was a natural entrepreneur, first launching a blackberry-picking and distribution operation, then building a lawn-mowing company—not to mention his forays into the proverbial hodgepodge of door-to-door sales. In each of these ventures, Marcus was the business "owner" who got other kids to do the work. No doubt about it, he'd wanted to run a business his whole life.

He did well in college, majoring in business and graduating with a 3.5 GPA. He played intramural sports to keep his athletic skills sharp and to keep the weight off from too much pizza and studying. After college he worked for a large corporation for three years and eventually applied to Northwestern, where he graduated with honors. Marcus felt like he was set for life. From here on in, things were only going to get better.

Most people would consider Marcus brash. Everyone who met him certainly liked him, but let's just say no one would accuse him of being short on ego. He had big dreams, knew where he wanted to go, and did everything he could to get there. He knew he had a lot going for him: He was smart, funny, and optimistic about the future. Today was a day to sit back and enjoy, along with his friends and family, where all his hard work had brought him—to a stellar platform from which to launch the next stage of his life.

As Marcus sat and pondered his future, a hand slapped him on the shoulder and a voice boomed, "So, what's next, Bigshot?" The hand belonged to Marcus's Uncle Fred, an insurance salesman like his brother, Marcus's dad.

"Not much, Uncle Fred. Maybe start and sell a few companies, get rich, buy a nice little island in the Caribbean, and then, oh, you know, take over the world. What do you think?"

Uncle Fred laughed that big booming laugh and tilted his head back. "If anyone could do, it would be you, boy. I always knew you were destined for greatness. Now that you got that fancy-pants degree, it's just a matter of time," he said. "Really, though, what's your plan?"

"Well, actually, most people who graduate from business school go on to become consultants, which I don't really want to do. I want to start my own business."

"Oh yeah, what kind?"

"I have an idea that I think could be really big, but it's gonna take some money to get it going."

"Lay it on me."

"Well, it's kind of complex, but basically it comes down to helping companies from America connect with businesspeople in other countries who are seeking invest-ments. I'd be putting the main players together and I'd also be able to use what I've learned about international currency trading. See, when money goes from one cur-rency to another, it loses a percentage in the exchange. I think that there are some ways to increase the efficiencies in the exchange. I think it would especially benefit non-profits that move billions of dollars around the world for things like disaster relief, mission projects, and things like that. I think I could potentially save organizations bil-lions of dollars."

"Wow, that sounds huge . . . and well over my head! It's not too big for you though. Go get 'em!" With that, he walked off, presumably to get another burger.

A long line of well-wishers made their way to Marcus throughout the afternoon. His cousins were slightly envi-ous and the older relatives were very proud. All in all, though, the family was thrilled for Marcus. It did feel a little weird to some of them, what with the whole MBA prestige thing going on—they had just never considered themselves "that" kind of family—but they were excited to see how high Marcus could soar.

At one point Jack pulled his brother aside. "What's going on, bro?"

"Not much. Just chillin'. What's up with you?"

"Just *eating!* Have you tried Aunt Susan's potato salad? It's awesome." That was Jack for you. Always about the food. Marcus was always about the money and Jack was always about the food. They had similar personalities and ran around together, but Marcus was just a little more, shall we say, focused. "In fact, I'm about to get some more. And maybe another plate of chicken wings. Want some?"

"No, I'm good. I have my fans to attend to!"

"Always the superstar," Jack said as he disappeared to get another plate.

All afternoon people had been piling gifts on a table near the sliding glass door that led into the kitchen; definitely one of the best perks of graduation. After everyone left the Drakes sat down to relax in the living room and watch Marcus open his gifts. Also joining them that evening was Margaret's mother, Beatrice, who was visiting from the little town in North Dakota where she lived. Marcus got the typical graduation gifts: travel kits, luggage, pens, stationery, and the like. His mom and dad gave him a very expensive briefcase that he had not so inconspicuously pointed out to his mother while on a trip to the mall the previous summer.

After all the other gifts had been opened, there remained just one. Beatrice got up and began to leave the room. "I will be right back. I left my gift in my room. I think you will like it." As she left, Marcus thought about his grandmother. He didn't know her all that well. His grandpa had died when Marcus was five and since she lived so far away and didn't like to travel, he hadn't seen her that often. As Marcus was growing up, he always thought Beatrice smelled like flowers. That really was the extent of it. That and the fact she always mailed him five bucks for his birthday, like virtually every grandmother in America.

At eighty, Beatrice took some time walking to the room she was sleeping in and back, and the family chitchatted in her absence.

"I bet she got you a bottle of cologne," Jack suggested. "Everyone knows you need it!"

"No, I am guessing a fingernail clipping set, which she should be giving to you instead. Do you ever cut those things? You look like a cougar."

"You boys better watch yourselves," Margaret interjected. "Your grandmother is going to surprise you."

"You know what she got me?" Marcus asked.

"I do. And it will be the best present you have ever received. I guarantee it."

"Really?" asked Jack. "Grandma came through for Marcus? Cool."

Just then Beatrice came slowly back through the door into the living room. While she walked a little slower these days, she was actually in good health, considering her age. She just walked slower than before. When it wasn't too cold out, she strolled around her small town to keep active. During the winter she did what she called "old people stretching" at the grange hall three days a week.

She didn't have a gift in her hand. Just an envelope. Marcus hoped it wasn't five dollars. As she got close to Marcus, she handed it to him and said again, "I really think you will like this. At least I hope you will."

This was the best gift ever? Marcus wondered. It couldn't be a huge check because he knew that his grandma didn't have that kind of money. What could it be? There was only one way to find out. He tore open the envelope and inside found a simple card that read:

A WEEKEND WITH BOBBY GOLD
JUNE 19–23

Along with it was a slip of paper with a phone number that said cell.

Okay, this was strange. Bobby Gold was *only* one of the most famous billionaires in America. Marcus was very aware of who he was, but what did the card mean? Margaret smiled softly as she watched Marcus's confused look.

"I don't get it, Grandma. Is it a seminar or something? Is he speaking somewhere? What do you mean by 'a week-end'?"

"I mean you will be spending the weekend—actually four or five days—with Bobby Gold. I arranged the whole thing." She was beaming now. Margaret and Bill also looked happy, while Marcus and Jack just looked quizzically at each other.

"Okay, so I must be really in the dark. How am I going to spend a weekend with Bobby Gold? And what am I going to do with him?" The thought crossed his mind that perhaps his grandma might be pulling his leg.

"Oh yes, I suppose it appears strange, doesn't it? I arranged for you to spend that time with Bobby so he could teach you a little about business. That should be fun, don't you think?"

"Well, sure, Grandma, it sounds great, but how did you pull this off?" He still wasn't sure it was actually true.

"I called him and asked him if he would do it for me," Beatrice said matter-of-factly.

"You just picked up the phone and asked a guy worth *eighteen billion dollars* if your grandson could hang out with him?"

"Exactly."

"Mom," Margaret said, interrupting their obviously confusing exchange, "perhaps you should explain how you know Bobby."

"Oh yes, that's a good idea. It sounds outlandish, doesn't it?"

"You know Bobby Gold," Jack and Marcus said in unison.

"I do. Well, more accurately, I did. You know me, I don't like to brag, so I never told you that I was Bobby's nanny for three years when he was growing up. From the time he was eight until he was eleven—such a nice young man. But I moved away when your grandfather got transferred for work and I didn't keep up with what had happened to him until I started reading about him and seeing him on television. He has become quite successful, you know."

"Of course I know." Marcus looked at his mom and dad. "Did you guys know that she knew Bobby Gold?"

"No, we knew she was a nanny for a little boy whose family had some money, but we never knew who it was. We didn't know until she asked if you would like this for a gift."

Marcus turned back to his grandma. "So, how did you get this arranged?"

"I called him up and left a message with his secretary and asked him to call me. The next day he did. I told him that you were graduating from Northwestern's business school and asked if he would spend some time with you. He remembered me—we always got along so well—and said he would be happy to do it. Then he looked at his schedule and suggested that you accompany him on a little trip he has planned. I checked with your parents and they said that you were free and so that is how it came to be. I thought you would like it."

"Grandma, I *love* it!" Marcus got up and went over to give his grandma a hug and a kiss to say thank you. She still smelled like flowers. "Thanks so much, Grandma. This is going to be awesome."

She squeezed him tight. "You are welcome, Marcus. I am so proud of you. You should be able to be as successful as Bobby has become."

Marcus stood up. "Well, let's start with my first million before we get to a billion—or eighteen." He turned to Jack. "Dude, I am going to be hanging with Bobby 'Nothing's Better Than Gold' Gold!"

BOBBY "NOTHING'S BETTER THAN GOLD" GOLD

Bobby Gold. How does one describe Bobby Gold? At age forty-seven and the tenth richest American, the press has used an endless amount of words to describe him. Some people might consider him arrogant, but that is far from the truth. Perhaps the best word to describe him is *flamboyant. Showy, colorful, loud,* and *flashy* would also work. *Modest* and *reserved?* Not so much. Above all else, though, Bobby Gold has an abundance of charisma and vision, an unparalleled work ethic, impeccable business acumen, and an amazing sense of timing.

He was raised by affluent parents who worked just outside Chicago. In many ways he was similar to Marcus. He started a string of businesses, played the same three sports, and also wanted to become a successful business-man. Unlike Marcus, he never finished college. He got into computers his sophomore year, and as soon as he saw the business potential he promptly quit school, much to the chagrin of his parents—at least until he started what would become the first major hit of his business career: Gold Hard Drives. The computer revolution was in full swing and what people really needed was more storage on their hard drives as games and applications got bigger and bulkier. Of course, many big companies were into the business but Bobby Gold dove right in like David to their Goliath and eventually took a major market share. When he took the company public at age twenty-six, he hit the jackpot for $750 million. Since then he had been on a twenty-one-year tear through the business world, diving into every industry that caught his eye: software, media companies, music labels, hotels, clothing, and the stan-dard billionaire luxury, a major league baseball team. Not to mention a plethora of other companies he owned that most people knew nothing about.

He branded all his products with the claim that "Nothing's Better Than Gold." It was brilliant, really—especially considering that his products were indeed the best on the market. He was true to his word. Even the hapless baseball team he bought ended up winning the World Series a few years after he took over.

Bobby Gold was not just rich and successful, but extraordinarily influential. He seemed to have a magic touch for achieving the seemingly impossible and was known for his tremendous ability to change people's minds and help them see his point of view. People often remarked that they left meetings with Bobby amazed that they'd ever disagreed with him in the first place. There was something about him that made people want to work with him, listen to him, and learn from him.

But perhaps what was most impressive about his influence was what he did with it. There are those who gain great wealth and then build their own little world, coming out only to gain more wealth for themselves. Then there are those who see wealth as a way to make an impact on the world around them. Though few knew it, Bobby was a huge humanitarian, helping charities not only in America but around the world. He sat on many boards of nonprofits and helped them not only with financial contributions, but with his expertise as well. One of the things he was proudest of was a huge micro-loan program he had started and financed that gave small low-interest loans, sometimes as little as fifty dollars, to thousands of impoverished people in South America and Africa, allowing them to buy farm animals and equipment to start their own businesses.

He had more than a few detractors, though, most of whom were jealous of his success. Bobby Gold loved to live large. He made a splash at every business launch by hiring big-name bands like the Rolling Stones to perform. He loved fast cars, boats, and jets. He skydived and went deep-sea fishing. He had six homes in the United States and three in Europe. Some people just didn't like Bobby Gold's style, and he had *lots* of style.

For all his flash, there was one thing he wasn't: a playboy. Sure, before he got married, he dated a few supermodels, but ultimately he settled down with a schoolteacher he met through a friend. They were perfect for each other. Susan let Bobby be who he was and didn't try to change him. In addition, she held down the fort with their three children while he set his sights on conquering the universe. Despite their hectic schedules, they still maintained a close relationship, which, of course, the media didn't cover. Why would they when they could show him shaking hands with a movie star instead?

Bobby Gold and the media had a give-and-take relationship and one thing was clear: They were both responsible for the "Nothing's Better Than Gold" brand. He dished it out, and they served it to the public. He was born with the perfect name for what he had accomplished. Everything he touched turned into, well, gold.

THE ART OF INFLUENCE

After dialing the cell number that came with the card his grandma had given him, Marcus spoke briefly with Bobby Gold. Bobby informed him that he would be at the airport to pick up Marcus at 3:30 p.m. on Thursday and they would leave shortly thereafter for New York for a meeting on Friday. They would be spending the night at his Park Avenue condo. Marcus just couldn't believe that he was actually talking with

Bobby Gold, let alone going to spend a few days with him. It was like a dream. Bobby had told Marcus to dress casually for the flight but to bring suits, both business and swim.

Around three o'clock, Jack and Marcus arrived at the small executive airport about ten miles away from the large international airport near their home. Going in and out of these smaller airports is one of the perks of the rich. No wait times, no standing around. No taking your shoes off and shuffling along waiting for your baggage to be scanned. Marcus was very much looking forward to it. He had been reading the luxury magazines for years and already had his eye on a car and a boat, but even with his big dreams, he hadn't gotten his brain around the cost of a private jet.

Jack and Marcus sat in the small terminal, waiting. Marcus's two bags sat by his side. One garment bag contained his suits and one standard bag held his other clothes.

"I wonder what kind of jet he has," Jack asked.

"A slick one, I guess. Probably a Gulf V, a Falcon, or a Challenger."

Jack chuckled as he said, "Wanna bet it's gold?"

"Hah! Probably!"

"Marcus?"

"Yeah, Jack?"

"Don't mess this up."

"I won't mess it up. What are you talking about?"

"Well, you know. You can be cocky sometimes. This dude's one of the richest guys in the world. I still can't believe you get to do this."

"Me neither, bro. Don't worry, I won't blow it. This is going to be so cool."

They sat there in silence for a few moments, then Marcus added, "Besides, I can probably teach him a thing or two. Who knows? After I'm done with him, he could move up a few notches on the Forbes 400 list."

"Yeah, I'm guessing that will happen whether he meets *you* or not."

Just then a woman from the terminal came over and told them that their plane would be there in about ten minutes. Jack and Marcus spent the time watching the sky, looking for the plane to appear. When it did they watched it all the way in until it landed, and they noticed a puff of smoke as the tires touched down. The plane soon came to a halt at the end of the runway, turned around, and started taxiing to the terminal.

Jack elbowed Marcus. "Told you it would be gold." And emblazoned across the fuselage were the words *Nothing's Better Than Gold!*

The airplane came to a stop just in front of the small terminal and the door opened outward, revealing the steps to board. Out walked Bobby Gold. He stopped on the top of the stairs and looked around like a king surveying his land.

Jack and Marcus walked out of the building toward the airplane. When Bobby saw them, he started a slow jog down the stairs and asked loudly, "Which one of you is my new apprentice?"

As they approached each other Marcus announced that it was he who would be spending the next few days with Bobby. "And this is my brother, Jack. He wanted to meet you so he drove me here. We have both been big fans for a long time." Bobby pumped their hands in a vigorous handshake.

"Absolutely great to meet you both."

"I am just so thankful for this opportunity, Mr. Gold. Thanks so much."

"First off, Mr. Gold is my dad. Call me Bobby. Second, it is my pleasure. It was great to hear from your grandmother again. She was my all-time favorite nanny. I often wondered what had happened to her, but I was so busy I never tracked her down."

"We didn't even know she knew you," Jack said.

"Yep, she was my nanny for three years. And those

three years were tough ones for my family, so she was there at a very important time. She was a total lifesaver. Poured a lot of love in my heart, your grandmother did."

Jack and Marcus glanced at each other. "That's awesome," Marcus said.

Bobby waved toward the plane. "Hey Jack, do you want to take a look at the plane before we get out of here?"

"Yeah, I would love that."

"Let's go," Bobby said as he began moving toward the plane. "This is my baby. Gets me everywhere I need to go. Care to guess what kind?"

"It's a Falcon," Marcus said.

"Very good." Bobby was impressed. "Most people guess that it's a Gulfstream, since that's the brand most people know. But you're right. It's a Falcon 900 EX. This baby is the way to go." As they went up the stairs he told them about the performance. "We cruise around 40,000 feet at about .82 of Mach speed. It has a range of about 4500 nautical miles, which gets me pretty much anywhere I want to go, nonstop. Burns about 300 gallons of jet fuel an hour."

"What does one of these go for?" Jack asked. Marcus elbowed him.

"Oh, don't worry, talking about money doesn't bother

me, Marcus. People are too afraid of talking about money. They think if you make a lot, you'll automatically think you are better than everyone else. Not true at all." He looked at Jack. "I think we got this for around forty million if I remember correctly. Plus or minus a little."

As they entered the plane Bobby pointed to the left, into the cockpit. "This is Joe and Ned. They are the best pilots in the world. Ned here can fly anything, Falcons, Gulfs, Challengers, helicopters . . . anything."

They turned into the plush seating area. "It has eight very comfortable seats here and a few pull-out tables. You saw the galley up front, which is also where the bathroom is." He walked to the back and pushed open a door in a wall. "And here's where I sleep. You wouldn't believe how well I can sleep in here. With all the traveling I do, it's essential."

"Very cool," Jack said.

"That's about it," Bobby said. "It gets me where I want to go. I thought about getting the new BBJ—the Boeing Business Jet—but decided against it. It's much bigger, but I just love this plane."

Jack and Marcus looked around some more, fiddling with the switches like schoolboys before they found themselves together on the tarmac again. It was time to go.

"Thanks for the ride, bro. See you in a few days."
Marcus gave Jack the standard man hug, handshake with
the right, reach around, pull close and slap of the back
with the left.

Soon the plane was rapidly climbing into the sky.

"So, what did you study at Northwestern?" Bobby
asked.

"The core stuff. Marketing, leadership, finance, en-
trepreneurship, etcetera. Are you familiar with the typical
business school curriculum?"

"A little. I am not very highly edu-ma-cated, you
know," he said, purposefully mispronouncing the words.
"I dropped out of college. It broke my parents' hearts.
But I suppose everything turned out all right," chuckling
as he said the last part.

"I'll say it did."

"Here's what I think, Marcus. Business school is
great, and from everything I hear, Northwestern has an
excellent program. Knowing that you graduated from
Kellogg tells me that you know the science of business,
but the way I see it, that's only half of it. Now I want to
teach you the other side of business, or as I call it, the *art*
of business."

"The art of business. I like the sound of that. But
what's the difference?"

"It's like this. A million bucks plus a million bucks is what?"

"Two million."

"Right. And it is *always* two million," Bobby said. "And if you make twenty percent on a hundred million, how much did you make?"

"Twenty million."

"Again, always. That's science. It's math. Business obviously has a major component of that, but it isn't the most important part. You graduated from a big class. You all got the same education. You all had the same teachers. You all lived in the same town. You basically had the same experience. You are all very smart and talented."

"Yeah . . ."

"So, it begs the question: What separates the successful from the unsuccessful? When you all come back for your twentieth reunion, some of you will have been very successful and others not so much—comparatively at least."

"Good question. I hadn't thought of that before. I guess it's hard work that separates the successful from the unsuccessful."

"Hard work is obviously going to be a big help. I work my butt off, believe me. But that isn't what I want to teach you on this trip. I want to teach you about influence. *Influence is the key to success.* Influence is the art of business."

"Well, that's a relief, since I can be pretty persuasive."

"I'm not talking about persuasion. I am talking about influence. I think there is a big difference between the two."

"How so?"

"Persuasion is about convincing people of something." Bobby got up and moved toward the galley. "You want a soda or water or something? Sometimes I have a flight attendant on board, but it's self-serve this time."

"Yeah, water would be great. Thanks."

"Persuasion is about what you do to other people. It is about techniques. How to win an argument, how to make a presentation, that sort of stuff. Now don't get me wrong. That's all good stuff to know. I think I am pretty persuasive when I want to be.

"Influence, on the other hand, is about you," he said as he handed Marcus a bottle of sparkling water.

"What do you mean, about me?"

"Influence is your ability to change another person's thoughts, beliefs, or actions. In order to be successful in business, you have to be able to influence people. You can't be a good salesperson and you certainly can't be a good leader if you don't know how to influence people. It is the core competency of both leadership and sales, the two major parts of business. So, how do you do it? Influence is all about who you become as you progress through life. You see, people don't do business with numbers or corporations. They do business with people. The kind of person you are is what determines your influence, which, in turn, is what determines your success."

"Well, I am a good person."

"I am sure you are, but how does that translate into what other people think? That's what matters."

"Perception is reality, right?"

"It is. And the best way to manage perception is for it to be real in the first place. So you have to *become* the type of person that others want to follow. You have to *become* the type of person that others want to buy from.

"Another way to look at it is this: You can't decide if you are going to be a leader. You can only decide if you will become the type of person others want to follow. Think about it. Who makes the decision whether any sale is going to take place?"

"The buyer."

"Correct. Who decides whether to follow someone else or not?"

"The follower."

"Correct again. So the buyers and followers are decision makers. Influence is a gift that they give to you. They let you influence them. They make that decision, not you. The only decision you make is what kind of person you will be. It is totally about your personal transformation into a great leader. That is the key, Marcus. I know you know the science of business. You couldn't have graduated from Northwestern if you didn't. But what you need to learn is the art of business—influence. It's all about people. It is about understanding the nuances and subtleties of human psychology and how people act toward you and react to you. And it is about your transformation into a person of influence."

"So how do I transform myself, as you put it?"

"Good question. We are all constantly in a state of transformation. Our lives are journeys—our professional lives as well as our personal ones. We all have experiences, both good and bad—we can't control that, but we can control how we respond to the things that happen to us. If we choose to get better, we become leaders. If we choose to get worse, we don't."

"Who would choose to get worse?"

"Nobody would describe it that way, but it happens all the time. People have stuff happen to them and they don't use it as a learning or growing experience. Instead, they freeze in their tracks, or they get afraid and stop the journey—and that is worse than anything that could have happened to them in the first place. People who succeed are always getting better."

"That makes sense."

"Look, most people would see me and my life and say that I have it made, that I was born with a silver spoon in my mouth, that I got lucky. What they don't realize is that every day for decades I have been making choices that have determined what type of person I would become. I have had to make many tough decisions. I have had hardships. People overlook them though. They just see the public persona, not to mention the boats, cars, and planes."

"So, what hardships have you experienced?"

"There have been a few that could have really derailed me. When I was a child my mom and dad were on the verge of divorce. There was a lot of tension at home, to say the least. Luckily Beatrice, your grandmother, was there. Still, that kind of thing can leave a mark on a kid. I can still vividly remember some of their battles. They were really scary. I was afraid my dad would leave us, that I would never see him again. To this day I have to make decisions to not let my childhood hold me back.

"And, I don't know if you remember this or not, but I started my first business, Gold Hard Drives, with my best friend. We got to a stage where business stalled out, mainly because he wouldn't grow—not as a person or as a leader. I knew we had enormous potential and he didn't want to do what it would take to grow the business."

"So what happened?"

"I bought him out. I didn't have a whole lot of cash, but I gave him as much as I could of my own, about $100,000, and then gave him as much cash as I could from the business and still operate. And then I gave him a small—very small—stake in the business that he could cash in if we ever had an IPO."

"That must have been good enough for him."

"No, at the time of the IPO he got about $2 million. I got $750 million. So he sued me. My best friend sued me."

"Whoa. What happened?"

"Well, he didn't get any more. It was obvious that I had built the company to what it was when we took it public. He had signed a buyout agreement and got what he had agreed to. I mean, when we parted ways, I could have run the business into the ground, but I didn't. I also took on a lot of risk to take it to the level I did."

"So where is he now?"

"I have no idea. He never spoke to me again. That was crushing. He had been my best friend since first grade.

His dad even called me once and told me that his son was being unreasonable and that they didn't hold anything against me. That was nice, I guess, but not the same."

Marcus nodded, and Bobby continued. "But possibly the most difficult time of my life was when my wife miscarried our first child. That hurt a lot. It was a terrible time for both of us. I still wonder what that baby would have been like." Bobby Gold, American icon and dynamo, allowed his gaze to drift off to the horizon outside the window. Marcus said nothing.

A few moments later Bobby broke the silence as he turned back to Marcus. "I didn't mean to be a downer. I just want to make it clear that bad things happen to everyone. It's how we respond to them that determines what kind of people we will become—and what level of influence we will have."

"I get it. But where do I start? What can I work on today?"

"Well, you have to work on yourself all the time. Certainly, negative experiences give us the biggest challenges to overcome, but we have to choose to learn and grow each and every day. Let me try out a little experiment on you."

CHARACTER AND SKILLS, VIRTUE AND TALENT

Bobby pulled a pen and paper out of a drawer to the left of their seats. "Okay, I want you to write down ten things you look for in a leader. Think about a great coach you played for or a boss you liked, anybody who influenced you in a positive way. What would you look for in a person that you would allow to influence you?"

Bobby got up to use the restroom while Marcus began working on his list.

When he got back, Marcus turned the list around for him to read.

1. Honesty
2. Passion
3. Vision
4. Empowering
5. Fairness
6. Decisiveness
7. Good listening skills
8. An ability to communicate
9. Courage
10. Positive attitude

"Great list," Bobby said. "These are things I would look for as well. Now, I do this little exercise with our executives all the time, so these are all words I've seen before. Take a look at them. Every single one of them can be classified as either a character trait or a skill. That's important. People are always looking at you and deciding, either consciously or subconsciously, whether or not they will follow you. And the two things they're looking at are your character and your skills."

"Okay."

"One of my favorite quotes comes from Thomas Jefferson. He said that there is a 'natural aristocracy among men, the grounds of which is virtue and talent.' You know what that means?"

"What?"

"It means anyone—*anyone*—can rise to the highest levels if they have virtue and talent or, as I put it, character and skills. That's how you get to the top. Now, take a look at those things you wrote down and take each one individually. Is each one a character trait or a skill?"

Marcus took a few moments and thought through each one and then announced he had eight character traits and two skills.

Just then Ned's voice came through the cabin and announced that they were about twenty minutes from touchdown in New York. Bobby picked up a handset from the side of his seat and pushed a button. "Ned, can you make sure we take a scenic route in? I want Marcus to get a good view of NYC at night."

Bobby turned back to Marcus. "It is beautiful at night. I love to see city lights from this view," he said. "But back to the matter at hand. Eight character traits and two skills. That sounds about right."

"What do you mean by that?"

"I have had thousands of executives do this exercise and it always comes out the same, right around seventy or eighty percent character traits, which proves my theory about who you are being the most important aspect of influence."

"So are you saying that skills aren't important?"

"No, not at all. You have to have both character and skills. Think about it this way: Would you be able to be a great leader if you had impeccable character but no skills?"

"No, of course not."

"That's right, nobody wants to follow someone who's all character and no skill. That kind of person might be a great friend, but not a leader," Bobby said. "And what if you have tremendous skills but no character? What are you then?"

"A politician?" Marcus said with a smile.

Bobby laughed out loud. "I love that! Certainly, we have our fair share of characterless politicians, don't we? You can lead for a while with great skills, but if you don't have character, eventually people will turn their backs on you and cease to do business with you. Ultimately, leadership, sales, and business are about trust. A follower must trust the leader. A buyer must trust the seller. No character, no trust.

"Most companies focus too much of their energy on

the skill side of business. Have you ever been to a skills-training workshop?"

"Sure."

"Have you ever been to a character-training workshop?"

"Uh, no."

"Exactly. Which is why so many people see their businesses tank. Or never get off the ground. They focus on their people's skills and neglect building their characters. A person might give a killer speech or know how to work a room, but without the character traits like the ones on your list, he or she is bound to fail. And if you have enough people in your company who lack character, they can take the entire business down with them. But more on that later.

"For now, know this. If you want to attract people of vision you have to be a person of vision. If you want to attract people who are passionate, you have to be passionate. If you want to attract people who are fair and honest and positive—"

Marcus cut him off and finished his sentence. "I have to be fair, honest, and positive."

"Good student," Bobby said, smiling. "The next few days I am going to teach you my own Four Golden Rules of Influence—the standards I expect all of my executives to live by. I have been living by them my whole life. Which reminds me, you know *the* Golden Rule, right?"

"Sure I do. 'He who has the gold makes the rules.'"

Bobby put his head in his hands histrionically. "Oh boy, I have a *lot* of work to do these next few days." He looked up. "You're joking right? You *do* know the real Golden Rule, don't you?"

"That's not it?"

Bobby noticed the sly smile on Marcus's face.

"Oh, I get it. You got me," Bobby said. "Well, prepare to learn a few more over the weekend. But in the meantime, let's stop talking and enjoy the scenery. I love this view."

As the Statue of Liberty became visible, Bobby's face brightened. "I have seen that woman a thousand times and she still brings a tear to my eye. Millions of people came here from all over the world to pursue their dreams. Do you realize what an amazing influence America has had in the world?"

"I guess so."

"We certainly aren't perfect and we have made many mistakes throughout history, but America has always been that city on the hill, that light of hope. It is a tremendous opportunity to live here, Marcus. You can be anything you want to be. You can become anything you want to become. You can do anything that you want to do.

"The way I see it, there are two types of people in this world any way you break it down, and we all have to choose which group we will belong to as we journey through this life. There are those who lead, and those who follow. There are those who set the agenda, and those who follow it. There are those who make a significant impact, and those who don't. There are those who design their lives and live them exactly as they choose, and those who drift aimlessly through life, allowing others to choose for them.

"We all fall into one of those categories or the other. If we learn how to be influential, we lead the kinds of lives that leave impact. If we don't, we will never live the kind of significant lives that we are all capable of living. I believe that any single person can lead an influential life if they choose to.

"Think about all the people who make our society great, the positive influencers: the Little League coach who every parent wants their child to play for; the high school teacher who inspires troubled kids to stay in school; the parents who raise children who go on to make a difference in society; the businessperson who improves the standard of living in her city; the local politicians who make hard choices and impact their region for decades.

"There are those who influence society and those who are influenced. Personally, I want to be a leader and make an impact. But it is up to you to decide which group you want to be a part of."

FISHING OR HUNTING?

When the plane landed, Marcus asked about his bags.

"Oh, don't worry about them. They will meet you at the apartment. I have some folks who will take care of that."

"Oh, okay. Great."

As soon as the door opened and they started down the stairs, Marcus noticed two large black Lincoln Navigators complete with tinted windows. Standing outside the back door closest to the airplane was a gentleman resembling a Secret Service agent. He wore a dark suit and tie and had some kind of communication device in his ear. Sitting in the passenger seat was an identically dressed man. In the second SUV sat two more, at least that Marcus could see.

As they walked to the Navigators, Marcus spoke. "Wow, I never thought about the fact that you would have security, but I guess it makes sense."

"Yeah, one of the downsides of this much money. There are lots of crazy people out there who write threatening letters and make weird phone calls. Sometimes they show up at events and public appearances. And for the most part, I'm not even involved in anything really controversial. It's just the money, I guess. I have a full security detail around my wife and kids too. They try to stay invisible and we try to live a normal life."

As the doors opened, running boards automatically unfolded from under the side and they stepped into the first Lincoln. They settled into two of the four captain's chairs that faced each other. "So how many guys are in the car behind us?" Marcus asked.

"Just two. Four altogether. But these four guys pack the strength of thirty regular guys. Two are former Secret Service, one is a former Navy SEAL, and one is a former Delta Force. I'm in good hands."

"I can see how all this would be a little weird, though."

"It does take some getting used to." By now the SUVs were rolling along on their twenty-minute drive to Bobby's apartment. The phone rang and Bobby answered it.

"Bobby Gold." He even sounded enthusiastic answering the phone. "Uh-huh. Sure, I'm interested. I'll have to take a look again at the numbers." A long silence. "Well, I'll tell you what, I'll put the ball in your court. I think we could maybe make something work. I could go either way. You just call me back if you are ready to deal." Another pause. "Okay, later."

Bobby put the phone down in its cradle. After looking out the window for a moment, he asked what Marcus thought was a strange question. "Marcus, do you hunt or fish?"

"Neither."

"Okay. If you had to choose between hunting and fishing, which would it be?"

"Hunting, definitely."

"Just what I thought."

"Oh yeah, why's that?"

"That's what almost all young aggressive guys pick. But it could be your downfall in business. If you want to influence people, you need to drop the rifle and think like a fisherman. Remember earlier tonight when I talked about the difference between persuasion and influence?"

"Yeah, sure."

"Well, the way I see it, persuasion is like hunting while influence is like fishing."

"I don't get it. What do you mean?"

"Well, think about it. What does an animal do when it's being hunted?"

Marcus thought for a few seconds. "It runs, I guess."

"Exactly. Now, think about sales. I have found that so many people lose sales and their basic ability to influence because they are hunters. They are on the prowl looking for something to bag. That is why the people they try to lead or sell to run away, both literally and figuratively. It's human psychology. Let me give you a few examples.

"I remember when I was young, twenty or so, I got invited to a 'backyard get-together.' Maybe you've had this happen to you. And when I get there, I realize that the whole thing was a ruse to get me to listen to a new business opportunity. Now, believe me, I've always been open to new business opportunities, but this just felt like an ambush, like I was being hunted."

"Yeah, that actually happened to me last year. Something similar, anyway."

"So you know what I mean."

"Actually, I have another example," Marcus said. "I just bought a new car. But before I did, I had narrowed it down to two cars. I could have gone either way, but one salesman just wouldn't take his teeth out of me long enough for me to really compare the two. So I just dumped him and went with the less pushy salesman."

"Car salespeople are renowned for that kind of thing. Of course, the really successful car salespeople aren't the kind of people who track you down and hunt you. Influence, at least long-term influence, is nothing like that. You may get the first sale as a hunter, but not the second, third, or fourth. But a person who influences by fishing, that's a different story. True influencers put other people at ease and let them feel that they are the ones in control. And they are in control, don't ever forget that. The whole psychology of the transaction changes when you think of it like that."

Marcus laughed.

"What's so funny," Bobby asked.

"But in fishing, the animal still dies."

Without missing a beat, Bobby replied, "Not true! Haven't you ever heard of 'catch and release'? There is no such thing as 'shoot and release.' " Marcus laughed again.

"Yeah, you got me there. I guess that's why you are the billionaire."

"And don't you forget it," Bobby said with a smile. The two men were enjoying a great rapport for two people who had just met each other a few hours earlier. Marcus couldn't believe how few pretensions the man had for someone so powerful.

"So, that phone call I just took," Bobby continued. "That was a great example of fishing rather than hunting. It was about a little company I'm considering buying. Young guy started it up, has done real well, and now wants out. It's worth right about what he is asking for it. It could be worth ten times that much in five years though. So you got the usual back and forth that goes on in any sale. I'm trying to influence him and he's trying to influence me. But here's the thing. In this situation, he's become the hunter and I have become the fisher. He is super-committed to making this deal happen, and he wants more than anything to close it. The more I sit back and show that I can take it or leave it—which I can—the more he pursues the deal. The more I fish, the more influence I have. I am just waiting for the deal to come to me."

"No offense, Bobby, but not everyone can afford to sit back and wait, you know? What do you do if you're not quite at that position yet?"

Bobby laughed. "Good point. But you don't need to

be sitting where I am to be a good fisherman. It helps, sure, but if you follow this advice, you'll get there, believe me. The way I see it, there are four things you have to have in order to fish successfully—or to have influence. You know what the first thing is?"

"Uh, I guess you have to have fish."

"Bingo! You have to have fish. And you know what the good news is? There are plenty of fish. Marcus, I could buy ten companies a year for the rest of my life and still not even scratch the surface of how many there are out there. If some employees don't want to work for me, there are others who are looking for just that kind of job and pay. If someone doesn't want to buy from me, there are others who do. So if you want to have influence, relax, don't get desperate. Hey, here's one for you. Did you ever have a girl in high school who broke your heart?"

"Sure, don't we all?" Marcus said with a smile.

"And what did your parents tell you?"

Marcus's eyes widened as he got it. "There are other fish in the sea!"

"That's right! And there were. Had you kept pursuing that girl, what would she have done? Run, that's what. Because you would have been hunting. Eventually, I am guessing, you had another girlfriend who mended your broken heart."

"Yep."

"So, second thing about fishing. You have to go where the fish are biting. Here's the fact. There are going to be people who you are going to try to sell to in your career, or lead for that matter, who just aren't interested in what you have to offer. For whatever reason, they just aren't interested. They're not hungry. But everyone gets hungry eventually. When you come to that point you can either push—hunting—or you can back off—fishing."

"Sounds good, but how?"

"Okay. I own a little insurance company out of Atlanta. Picked it up a couple of years ago. What are you, twenty-six, twenty-seven years old?"

"Twenty-seven."

"Great. You aren't married, no kids. You don't need life insurance right now. At least, not much, if any. So an insurance guy corners you and starts the sales pitch. What do you tell him?"

"I'm not interested."

"That's right. You don't want to drop a bunch of money every month right now because you've got school bills, car payments, and no job. You're just beginning your career, and you have no responsibilities to speak of that you have to cover with life insurance. In other words, you aren't hungry, right?"

"Right."

"Now, that agent has a choice. He can press you hard and tell you why you are wrong, why you really do need life insurance, and become a hunter. What happens then?"

"I run. I stop answering the phone when he calls."

"Exactly. And he loses any chance he has to influence you and your purchasing decision later on in life. Now, as a burgeoning businessman with big dreams, eventually you are going to pay a lot for insurance to cover and protect all the wealth you are going to accumulate. You don't even want to know what I spend on insurance on myself and all my businesses each year!"

Marcus was getting it now. "So. If he wants my business eventually, he has to fish, not hunt."

"Right. He has to choose to fish. He has to sit on the side of the bank and wait for you to get hungry. Or go fish another hole. Eventually though, you will get married and have kids, earn a great income, and pile up assets. At that point you are going to need insurance."

"So how does he fish in the meantime?"

"Easy. He keeps the relationship open by staying in contact with you from time to time. He just keeps his line in the water waiting for you to get hungry. He doesn't jump in the river and go spear fishing!

"So, number one, you've got to have fish, and number two, you've got to wait until they are hungry. The third thing about fishing is the most important: *You have to use the right kind of bait.* I have a retreat house up in Montana on a river where there is some great fishing, but whether you're fishing in a river, lake, or the ocean you have to use the right kind of bait. If I go down to the river, pull out my rod and reel, and put a tin can on the hook, I will never catch a fish. I have to use the right kind of bait. For some fish you use fish eggs. For others you use minnows. Others you can use little rubber frogs. Others you can catch with tied flies. In every situation, though, you have to present bait that is *appealing* to the kind of fish you are trying to catch. It has to be attractive and alluring so as to draw the fish to you."

Just then the phone rang again. "Hold on a minute," Bobby said as he picked it up. "Hey, honey, can I call you back a little later when I get settled in? Great. Love you.

"Now, here is the key, Marcus: *You are the bait.* Many people simply do not understand this. It's not so much whether we have all the answers or can make a slick and persuasive speech or handle a person's objections that determines whether or not we will develop ourselves into successful influencers. It's who we are that makes us attractive to others. Ultimately, people are not buying your products, services, arguments, ideas, or visions for the future. They are first and foremost buying *you*. So the question you have to ask yourself is 'What kind of bait am I?' "

"So how do I become better bait?"

"That goes back to some of the stuff we talked about earlier. You improve your character and your skills. But I will tell you more when I get to the Four Golden Rules in the next couple of days."

"Awesome. I can't wait to hear them."

"The last important factor in fishing is *presentation*. How we present our bait is absolutely crucial to making a catch. Presentation only becomes important once you have the right kind of bait, never before. You can shine up a tin can till it sparkles and the fish still aren't going to bite. But once you have the right bait, then it all boils down to presentation. For some fish you can just throw the line in and let it sit. For other fish you throw it out and reel it immediately back in. And then there is fly fishing with its methodical and entrancing back and forth motion, almost like a dance. In every instance, success all boils down to presentation.

"If you're not careful, a bad presentation can kill your business. I was speaking at a conference sponsored by a large financial institution not too long ago when a guy came up to talk after my speech. He was, to say the least, an interesting sight. He hadn't learned the lesson of presenting himself. Well, I take that back. He had *mostly* learned the lesson, but not enough. When you looked at him from the floor up, you started out with beautiful dress shoes. Next came a perfectly tailored blue suit with a faint white pinstripe. He was very fit, so the suit hung well on him. His red tie complemented his suit perfectly. He was a good-looking young man with a square jaw. Up to this point he had a very impressive presentation. Unfortunately, he had a real hair problem. His hair was cut short, maybe an inch and a half in length. He had it bleached bright white with peroxide, heavily gelled, and pulled into about fifty points all across his head.

"I am sure he was probably a great young man. But what he didn't realize was that what people saw was a man in a business suit with the hairstyle of a teenager. His presentation hurt his ability to influence others to the degree that he could."

"He obviously didn't make much of a first impression on you, did he?"

"He made a first impression on me all right, just not the kind he needed to. First impressions count."

"But they say that you can't judge a book by its cover.

Just because someone has a weird hairdo doesn't mean he or she has a bad business sense."

"Okay, but we're talking about influence here, right? In order to succeed you have to be able to gain and keep influence with others. You are right that you can't judge a book by its cover. There is no way to tell what is on the inside of a book by looking at the cover. It could be filled with great information; it could be blank pages. But people *do* judge books by their covers all the time. It is human nature. We meet hundreds of people, all of whom want to do business with us, and we have to filter out the ones who are worth our time, money, and energy. So how do we do it? We make snap judgments. They're not always accurate, but we do it out of necessity. So my response is that if we want to do business and be successful, we have to make a good first impression. It is how we present ourselves to the world around us. In doing so, we don't erect barriers to them opening the book and going deeper."

Just then the Navigators came to a stop in an underground parking garage beneath the apartment complex. Marcus followed Bobby out and they took the elevator up to the apartment. They spent the rest of the evening eating dinner, getting to know each other a bit more, and watching a baseball game on the television. As the night ended, Bobby psyched Marcus up for the next day.

"All right, the bus leaves at seven a.m. sharp. Put on your best suit and your game face. You'll be flying wingman on a potential fifty-million-dollar deal in the morning."

Marcus went into his bedroom and there indeed were his bags, just as promised. He didn't even see who had brought them up. Of course, there was enough room for an army to fit in Bobby's apartment. At four bedrooms, six baths, and eight thousand square feet, this was more like a mansion than a regular old apartment. Ah, Marcus thought, it is good to be a billionaire.

GOLDEN RULE OF INFLUENCE NUMBER ONE: LIVE A LIFE OF UNDIVIDED INTEGRITY

At eight-thirty a.m. sharp, after having left Bobby's apartment exactly at seven for an early breakfast, Bobby, Marcus, and the security team from the Lincolns arrived at their destination: a relatively small company that Bobby was thinking of taking a stake in, in the hopes of growing it. The CEO's admin told them that her boss had been caught in traffic and was just a few blocks away. In the meantime, she led them into the conference room be-tween the CEO and CFO offices.

The boardroom had a classic high-powered look. It had beautifully ornate furniture and a killer view—the kind that is hard to come by in the concrete jungle. When Bobby and Marcus entered the room they were quickly greeted by the CFO, who asked them to sit down. The admin asked Bobby and Marcus if they would like some juice and danish.

"No, thank you," Bobby replied.

"None for me either, thanks."

They launched into the basic "getting to know you" chitchat for a few moments while the three of them waited for the CEO to arrive. During a lull in the con-versation, the admin came back in and spoke to the CFO.

"Laura Jackson called. She wants to know when she will get the package that includes the business plans and strategic overview?"

"Oh, I forgot to mail it! Do me a favor. Tell her I mailed it yesterday. Then overnight it to her today. Tell her she should get it tomorrow."

"Will do," she said before disappearing through the doors again.

"I hate when I forget to do things," the CFO said as he turned to Bobby. "I must be getting old."

A few minutes later the CEO entered the boardroom, apologizing for his tardiness. He asked the CFO if he had the financial sheets available.

"Sure do," he said as he handed Bobby and Marcus a short stack of papers. "The top two sheets are the overview, the next ten sheets have all the details."

Bobby turned to Marcus. "Give those a once over, will you? Let me know if anything pops out at you." Marcus began to delve into the paperwork. He loved this. Barely out of business school and here he was sitting at the right hand of one of the biggest movers and shakers in the world, helping him decide whether or not to go through with a deal. Who would have thought? As he started through the paperwork, he also tried to keep an ear to the conversation. Bobby was grilling the C-level duo on their past, present, and future. Bobby was known for his keen intuitive sense of which deals were right and which ones were wrong. Sure, he looks at the numbers, but he trusts his gut a lot, as well.

After about twenty minutes of give-and-take, Bobby thanked them for their time and told them that he would get back to them by the end of the day. One-day decisions may seem like a quick turnaround on a fifty-million-dollar deal, but in the overall scheme of Bobby's wealth, it was a pretty minor decision. Bobby had attended the meeting himself only because the CEO was a friend of a friend and he also thought it would give Marcus some action.

They discussed the meeting on the car ride back. "So, what did you think?" Bobby asked Marcus.

"It was great. I can't think of a better way to get my feet wet."

Bobby spoke to the driver. "Larry, can we hit a Starbucks? I'll have the usual." He turned to Marcus. "Anything for you?"

"Sure, a tall black drip."

"Got it," Larry said from the front.

"So, Marcus, let's see what Northwestern did for you. How did those numbers look to you?"

"I thought they looked really good." He was a little bit hesitant. They really did look good, but he just hoped that Bobby thought the same thing. He didn't want to end up on the wrong side of the fence right off the bat, missing some crucial piece of information. He wanted to impress Bobby. "What did you think?"

"I agree. The financials look very good. This fifty million could turn into four or five hundred million in six or seven years."

"So, are you going to do it?"

Just then the Lincoln pulled over for Larry's run into

the Starbucks. "Well, let's talk about it a bit. We know the science works, right?"

"The science?"

"Yeah, remember? The science and the art? The science is the numbers. Those work on this deal. What about the art?"

"Oh, yeah. Well, the two guys seemed sharp. They seemed like they knew what they were doing. They had a plan for expansion. What did you think?"

"I think you just had a great example of Bobby Gold's First Golden Rule of Influence."

"Okay . . ." Marcus didn't get where Bobby was going with this.

"Those two guys were trying to influence me to put *fifty million dollars* of my money into their business, right? Which means I'd have to hold them to my Golden Rules of Influence. Unfortunately, their CFO broke rule number one before the meeting ever began."

Larry climbed back into the Lincoln and handed the coffees to Bobby and Marcus. "Thanks, Larry. You got some for the rest of the guys, right?" Bobby kept the drivers flush with loaded Starbucks cards so they could always hit the coffee shop and buy for everyone.

"I sure did, thanks!" Larry said as he pulled back into traffic.

"So, what's rule number one?" Marcus asked.

"Right, back to the task at hand." Bobby placed his cup into the cup-holder as they swerved into traffic. "Golden Rule of Influence Number One is: *Live a life of undivided integrity.*"

"I don't get it. Those guys didn't have integrity? How do you know?"

"I'm all about the small stuff, Marcus. If people are willing to break the rules when it comes to the small stuff, then it is just a hop, skip, and jump to the big stuff. You say the numbers look great, and they do—if they are true."

"Why wouldn't they be true?" Marcus was confused.

"Because the CFO could have lied about them."

"What makes you think he would lie about the numbers?"

"Think, Marcus. Remember the interaction between the CFO and the admin before their CEO arrived?"

"About the package?"

"Yes, about the package."

Marcus thought through the conversation again and then it hit him. "He asked his admin to lie for him! But I don't know if that means he would lie to you."

"That's the problem. I don't know if he is willing to lie to me or not. But I do know that he is willing to lie.

He has no integrity—he has a divided life. Maybe he's truthful most of the time, but he's already proven that some of the time he isn't. People like that are always driven by personal expediency. They tell the truth if it's convenient for them to do so. So what is to keep their CFO from fudging the numbers a bit with me? Maybe hiding a crucial detail that might cause me problems later on?"

"I don't know," Marcus said. He just didn't see it that way.

"Marcus, let me tell you about integrity. It is *all* you have. It is the foundation of everything else you do. Without it, you are lost in business. Ultimately the relationship between leader and follower, between buyer and seller, is about trust. Without integrity, it is impossible to trust. And whether you are dealing with fifty dollars, fifty million dollars, or five hundred million dollars, it is imperative that you have trust."

"Yeah, I agree with that. But what do you mean by an undivided life or however you put it?"

"Okay, go back a few years to high school math. Think about a term that shares the same root word with integrity."

"Integer?"

"Very good. Now, what *is* an integer?"

Marcus paused. "Got me there. What is it again?"

"A whole number," Bobby answered. "So, basically, having integrity means living a whole life. You are wholly truthful. If you are willing to lie, then you have divided yourself and given up your integrity. You have the truthful part, but you also have the lying part. The problem then is that the person whom you hope to have influence with now has a dilemma: Which one of you is speaking at that moment, the honest person or the liar?"

"With all due respect, it sounds like you expect people to be perfect. We all make mistakes."

"I agree wholeheartedly, Marcus, and that is a very good point. I have made more than my fair share of mistakes. Let me give you another example, though. About six years ago I bought a large Texas concrete contractor. They do big jobs like highways and shopping malls. They gross around two billion dollars a year. I've spent some time with them and noticed that they use the word *integrity* as it relates to concrete. They have to make sure that the concrete maintains its integrity. In fact, if you think about it, structural engineers use the term *integrity* all the time. Think about the small cracks that develop in a structure. Even though they happen all the time, they're something to be concerned with."

"So the small cracks are the breaks in our integrity?"

"Exactly. Everybody has these small cracks. The key is to be aware of them so we can fix them before they grow. Let me ask you this: Do you think that followers expect their leaders to be perfect?"

"No, I don't."

"They don't. But—and this is a big but—they do expect their leaders to admit and correct their mistakes, mend the cracks in their integrity, if you will. Left unchecked, eventually a lack of integrity erodes the trust that is needed between a follower and a leader. Little cracks don't bring down businesses, big cracks do. Little cracks don't bring down marriages, big cracks do. But do you know what the problem is with little cracks?"

"What?"

"They grow up to be big cracks. Marcus, the best thing you can do for yourself, for your business, for the family you will eventually have, is to always lead a life of undivided integrity. That is rule number one for living a life of influence. So be aware of yourself and your integrity at all times. When you find yourself with a crack—or if someone points one out to you—be sure to deal with it. Don't let it go."

"Well, I guess I have cut a few corners in my time. But I always thought I had integrity."

"Everybody *thinks* they have integrity. Go to a prison

and everyone there will tell you they have integrity. The problem is that we give ourselves more charity that we give others. What we think is a small mistake, others consider a lack of integrity. You ever read Aristotle?"

"Aristotle?"

"Yeah, Aristotle."

"One time in college. I don't even remember what he wrote though."

"In *Rhetoric*, Aristotle wrote about influence and persuasion. He said that there were three parts to it: logos, pathos, and ethos. Logos is logic. You have to be logical. You have to make sense. Pathos is passion. You have to be passionate. Some people are so logical and their lack of enthusiasm puts people to sleep. Some people are so passionate about their beliefs but make no sense. You have to have both. But, what holds them both up is ethos, and that of course is . . ."

"Gotta be ethics."

"Ethics. Exactly. If you want to have influence, you need a foundation of ethics on which your logic and passion can stand."

"And you wonder about that CFO's ethics."

"Right."

"So, are you going to do the deal with them?"

"Have you ever had someone lie to you so that it affected your business with them?" Bobby replied, answering the question with a question.

"Let me think."

"Five minutes out," Larry announced from the front seat.

Marcus slapped his hand on his leg. "Yeah, as a matter of fact, I did. I was buying a new computer for college and caught the salesman in a lie about the computer's capabilities. I walked out and went to the computer store down the street. I even paid eighty bucks more for the computer."

"That's my point exactly. So, what is the takeaway in all of this? Make it your absolute goal to live a life of integrity. Make it your goal to have others consider you a person of your word. You do that by living with integrity. Doing so is the foundation of leading an influential life. Not doing so is the kiss of death."

"So, you aren't going to do the deal?"

"No, of course not. That CFO told a fifty-million-dollar lie. I'll call the CEO later and let him know."

Marcus looked out the window as they approached the airport. He was thinking about whether or not he had any small crack he needed to fix.

"All right, test time," Bobby said. "Golden Rule of Influence Number One?"

Marcus snapped to attention. "Live a life of undivided integrity. Got it."

"Great. Let's jump on the plane."

"Where are we going?"

"Chicago, man. Big game tonight. We can't miss it."

"But all my stuff. It's still at the apartment."

"No it isn't. It's all on the plane," Bobby said with a smile. "Let's go. I can't wait for you to meet Tom Martin."

GOLDEN RULE OF INFLUENCE NUMBER TWO: ALWAYS DEMONSTRATE A POSITIVE ATTITUDE

Tom Martin had the highest winning percentage of any major league manager—and for good reason. His players loved him and gave every bit of effort they could. It certainly helped that he had a great baseball mind, but it was impossible to find a person who had a bad word to say about him, and that served as the basis for his reputation.

Tom had been out of baseball for a couple of years when Bobby Gold picked up the phone and invited him back in. Tom had begun a new career as a broadcaster, had written a book, and was trying to spend more time with his family, something that had been tough to do as a coach and manager, with a schedule of 162 games a year, not including spring training and the playoffs. But Tom's youngest child had left for college the same year that Bobby had purchased his beloved, albeit hapless, Chicago baseball team, so the timing was right.

Bobby had followed Tom's career closely and knew that he embodied his second Golden Rule of Influence: Always demonstrate a positive attitude. So he picked up the phone to find out if the timing was right for Tom to jump back into the big leagues. Indeed it was, and he quickly turned the team around. He, along with the general manager, made some good strategic trades and began to rebuild their minor league clubs to prepare for the future. Soon, the team had its first winning season in over two decades. Tom Martin was *back!*

As Bobby and Marcus walked into the manager's office deep in the stadium, Marcus was wide-eyed. He loved baseball and never dreamed he would be offered this kind of opportunity, especially so early in life. Heck, he was happy if he got tickets where he could see the team without binoculars. Now he was meeting with one of the legends of baseball. It was going to be great fun and an honor. He couldn't quite figure out how it fit into the lessons on influence he was supposed to be getting, but he wasn't going to argue.

"Marcus," Bobby began, "meet Tom Martin, the best manager in baseball."

"Great to meet you," Tom said, extending his hand.

"Fantastic to meet you!" Marcus exclaimed.

Tom motioned to some large leather couches in his office. "Let's sit down and talk for a bit. We've got an important game tonight so I don't have a ton of time, but Bobby told me he wanted us to spend some time together. He thinks you have a lot of potential. Since you're a graduate of Northwestern, I bet he is right. You have to be talented to make it there."

"Thank you," Marcus said.

Bobby knew they didn't have a lot of time so he stayed quiet and let Tom take the lead. Bobby had already prepped him on what he wanted him to discuss with Marcus. "So, you have been learning Bobby's Golden Rules of Influence, have you?"

"Well, one so far."

"All right, here is number two. You know, professional sports has changed a lot since the early eighties, let alone the fifties. We're talking big money now—and even bigger egos. Everyone is a walking corporation with built-in marketing departments, endorsement deals, investments, you name it. It used to be that the manager had the power and the players followed along. But as the players became richer and more important, they began to take the power out of the manager's hands. It isn't uncommon for a few players on a team to make up to five or six times what the coach does. In some cases it can be fifteen or twenty times. So the leadership dynamic has really changed.

"A team now will take the side of the player over the coach because they have twenty million dollars a year wrapped up in him while they have only a million a year in the coach. And fans aren't buying jerseys with the coach's name on it—they buy the player's jersey. So you can see where the loyalties lie. Occasionally you get an owner like Bobby who has his head screwed on right and doesn't cater to the prima donnas. He lets me do my job and because of him I'm allowed to make my own decisions about what I think will produce a winning team. This may be a game, but it is also Big Business with a capital *B*." He looked at Bobby. "How much do you have tied up in the team?"

"About half a billion dollars in all, and then over a hundred fifty million a year budget."

"As I said, Big Business. So, here I am, the leader and

influencer. I lead a team just like you will in the corporate world someday. I have followers. What makes it difficult for me is that every one of the people I am supposed to be influencing is used to being the leader. By the time these kids get to me they have been stars at every level for most of their lives. So how am I supposed to influence them? There are lots of different theories. I have my own, and it fits with Bobby's. And, quite frankly, if you go to the baseball record books and look at winning percentages, I feel comfortable with the idea that my philosophy works.

"There are different theories on how to influence others to follow you. Mine is simple: Always demonstrate a positive and optimistic attitude. That is how I influence these superstars I have to lead."

"And it works?" Marcus asked.

"It is basic human nature. Not only does it work in baseball, it works in business, it works in your marriage, with your kids, and in your life in the community. People want to be around positive, optimistic people. People *follow* positive, optimistic people. Do you like being around negative people?"

"No, of course not."

"Do you respond well to a good old-fashioned tail whoopin' when you fail?"

"Not really."

"Nobody does. And yet we have leaders who don't get it. They don't realize that if they become a positive and optimistic person, their leadership grows as their followers respond. I have players from other teams tell me all the time that they would love to play for me. I could carry two hundred players if the league would let me. Gaining and maintaining influence is all about understanding psychology. You have to understand what people are looking for and what they will respond to—and people respond to optimism."

"So how does that look in practical terms? How does it play out in real life? How do you remain positive and optimistic when things go wrong?"

"Good question. In life, stuff goes wrong. In baseball, we make mistakes. A great hitter will bat .350. That would put him up there for the batting championship every year. That means, though, that sixty-five times out of one hundred, that batter will march right back to the dugout rather than getting on base. Now, when most people have something go wrong they ask the same question: *Why?*"

"Is that a bad question?" Marcus asked.

"Not if it is an analytical question. We should ask why something has failed or gone wrong. But most people aren't asking why in that manner. They are asking 'Why did this happen to *me?*' or 'Why did this have to happen *now?*' or, my favorite, 'Why does this *always* happen?' They are focusing on the negative. They are lamenting their situation. And it gets them nowhere."

"So what *should* they do?"

"They need to ask the positive and optimistic question: *What good can come from this?* That question will help you focus on solutions. It will focus you on a better future. And bringing people to a better future is what influence is all about. Optimism is a choice that we make. In fact, here is a good way to remember optimism. The root word is *opt* and that triggers two thoughts. I teach this to all my players. If you opt to do something, you choose to do it. So optimism is a choice. No matter what the circumstances are, each player—or in your field, employee—has a choice to make about what their attitude will be. When something negative happens they can choose to react negatively and spiral downward, or they can choose to react with a positive and optimistic attitude and do better the next time.

"The second thing *opt* reminds me of is one of our team doctors. We have an ophthalmologist who works with our players and keeps their eyes healthy. He works with how they see. So optimism is about how you see the world around you. Put the two together and it all comes down to choosing to see the world in a positive way. You are choosing to believe that something good can come from negative circumstances and that the future will be better than the present. That's the kind of attitude people want to follow. They want leaders who see a brighter future."

"So how do I become that kind of leader?"

"I will share with you one simple piece of wisdom. If you remember it, I guarantee it will change you and those who follow you."

"What is it?"

"It's an old proverb I learned in Sunday school as a high schooler. I took it to heart and consider it to be the basis on which I have built an amazing life. It has helped my career, my marriage, and my kids. The old proverb says that 'the tongue has the power of life and death.' In other words, everything we say has a tremendous impact on ourselves and others. The words we use have the power to breathe life into people, and if we're not careful, death. Do you remember that old saying, 'Sticks and stones will break my bones, but words will never hurt me'?"

"Sure."

"Who in the world came up with that? It's totally

false. You break an arm and six weeks later you're good to go. Yet we meet people all the time who had someone say something negative to them twenty years ago that still effects how they live their life on a daily basis. Words have a tremendous power."

"How so?"

"First for ourselves. Don't forget the power we have to influence ourselves. When you make a mistake you should never start telling yourself negative things. Those negative words produce negative thoughts and actions. For us, it is a player who strikes out and then tells himself he can't hit in the clutch. Guess what happens? From that point on, he can't hit in the clutch. For your situation it may be a person who botches a presentation and then tells herself that she can't speak in front of others. She'll never move up because she can't lead from the front of the room. Negative words produce negative results. Positive words produce positive results. So I teach people how to take control of their minds and thoughts and the words they say to themselves."

"I bet not many managers do that these days."

"Some managers have such little control or understanding that they scream and yell and cuss their players out when they fail. That just exacerbates the problem. It has no positive influence. Players get hurt and bitter and negative. You, of course, know the name Carlos Menendez?"

"Sure, best hitter in baseball today."

"Well, he was when he came into the league, too. Then he hit a slump that lasted a couple of months about three years ago. He was playing for another team and I know the manager he had at the time. That guy chewed Carlos out endlessly, shaming him for his slump, and that just made it worse. Eventually management got sick of paying him for poor performance and traded him to us for a song. I knew that I could talk him into being the best hitter in baseball again, and I did. He just needed someone to believe in him and pump up his confidence. I told him over and over again that he is the best hitter in baseball and that is exactly what he has become.

"Now, some may say, 'Those guys are getting paid millions a year so they need to suck it up. You shouldn't have to stroke their egos.' But what we have to understand is successful people are still people, and all people react negatively to negative words. I have met business leaders all over America who have all the business skills in the world and no people skills. They can't keep good people because good people don't want to get beat up all the time. Let me give you another example. Are you married?"

"No."

"Girlfriend?"

"Not currently, but I've had a few."

"Okay, so let's say your girlfriend has just gotten her hair done and when you see her for the first time, you say, 'What happened to your hair?' How will she respond?"

"Yeah, not good," Marcus said with a smile.

"But how would she react if you came in and said, 'Wow, you look *gorgeous!*' "

"She would be very happy, I guess."

"Indeed she would. And I would suggest you don't follow that up with 'How much did that cost me?' " All three men laughed out loud. "You see, the words we speak have power. As leaders it is our job to speak life into those who follow us. We have people show up on our doorsteps from all sorts of backgrounds. Some have positive backgrounds and many have not-so-positive backgrounds. Either way, we lead people to a better future by being positive and optimistic, especially through the words we speak. We have to be positive in everything we do. I truly believe this will change your life, Marcus. It certainly has mine."

"And mine as well," Bobby chimed in.

Just then the first-base coach popped his head in the room. "Time for the meeting, Skipper."

"Ah, yes, baseball calls. I would love to keep talking, but I have to keep this guy happy with wins," Tom said as he pointed a thumb in Bobby's direction.

They all stood up, and Bobby and Marcus began heading out the door. As they left, Marcus thanked Tom for his time and the lessons he taught him.

That night, for the first time ever, Marcus sat in the owner's suite, a far cry from the outfield seats he had known as a child. He could get used to this. There was all the food he could fill himself with and the best seat in the house, right behind home plate. Not to mention how cushy those seats were! The men had a great time talking baseball and watching the game. Bobby was just young enough to be a friend to Marcus, and just old enough to be a mentor. He was enjoying this as much as Marcus was.

In the middle of the fifth inning Bobby finished his soda and peanuts and turned to Marcus. "Are you ready for the third Golden Rule of Influence?"

Marcus was a little surprised that the lessons would continue through the game, but was ready. "Sure."

Bobby stood up. "Let's go," he said, turning toward the door of the suite. And off they went.

GOLDEN RULE OF INFLUENCE NUMBER THREE: CONSIDER OTHER PEOPLE'S INTERESTS AS MORE IMPORTANT THAN YOUR OWN

As they walked down the private corridor, Bobby began the next lesson. "Marcus, ultimately business is *always* about the relationships. You have to learn how to create, develop, and maintain healthy relationships. If you can do that, you can do anything you want. You will have all the influence you need to achieve your dreams. Let me tell you a story about my uncle Walt. He's my mom's brother. Walt taught me at a young age one of the most important lessons about influence—and for selling and leadership, for that matter. When I was still a kid Walt sold tractors in the Midwest. And, boy, did he sell tractors. He was the best salesman in the best dealership in his town. So one day I asked him what the key to his success was. I figured the tractors he sold must be better than the competition. It wasn't that. So I guessed the price must be better. Not that either. I guessed the warranty. Nope, not that. Had to be the service. I had struck out on four guesses. I finally just asked him to tell me. You know what he said?"

"What?"

Bobby stopped in the hall and turned to Marcus. "He looked me right in the eye and smiled and said, 'Bobby, it all comes down to this: *My customers like me better than the other guy.*' That was it. People *liked* my uncle Walt. In fact, he was about the most likable guy I ever met. Don't get me wrong. He knew tractors and could close a deal, but more than anything else, people liked him. People do business with people they like. Period. So the question we have to ask ourselves is, 'Am I likable?' "

"I think I am likable."

"I think you are too, Marcus." They started walking again. "Do you know what makes people likable?"

"They're friendly."

"Yes, and they smile. They laugh. All the basics. But mostly, likable people all seem to get the Golden Rule of Influence: Consider other people's interests more important than your own. You see, we live in a world where most people are looking out for number one. They are interested in getting, not giving. I have found that success comes from looking out for the people who work for you by being interested in them and what they're involved with. That's why I am taking you on my rounds."

"Your rounds?"

"Yes, whenever I am here at the ballpark, I make sure to make the rounds and talk with the good people who work for me to make sure everything is going well. When you invite forty thousand people over for a shindig, you have to make sure everything is all right."

As they spent the next forty minutes walking around the stadium Marcus saw real life leadership at work. Bobby was a man of the people, even though he was one of the richest men in the world. "You've probably heard of 'leadership by walking around,'" Bobby said, "but what matters is *what you do* when you walk around. I make sure that I am looking out for my people and building relationships. I make sure they know that I care about them and am interested in them."

In fact, Marcus noticed that Bobby *never* brought up

anything work related with the people he stopped to talk to—at least fifty people in all. If they brought up a work situation Bobby would discuss it, but mostly, Bobby asked them about their lives, families, and hobbies. He would talk to the ushers about their wives. He talked to the peanut salespeople about their kids. He talked to the maintenance people about their weekend plans.

In between conversations, Marcus asked Bobby why this worked. "Well, because most bosses, especially rich and powerful bosses, walk around and look for things that are wrong and need attending to. Their workers dread their visits because of it. I think people enjoy seeing me come around. They know that I care about them."

"So you never correct anyone or point out poor work?"

"Oh, if I notice something, I'll talk to a manager about it and suggest they check on it. They manage. I lead. I want ultimate influence here. Sure, being the owner gives me a title, but I want *real* influence—the kind of influence that works when I am not here. I want people to like, respect, and admire me so that they take pride in their work and do a fantastic job. And it works. Since I took over the team from an owner who never left his suite, our stats on fan satisfaction have skyrocketed. That comes from the experience that our employees give people. Our people work hard because they know that their leaders care about them. That's human nature.

"Let me give you another example. Even though she doesn't have to work, my teenage daughter works at a local coffee shop. She and my wife had been going there for some time and she wanted to work there. It wasn't a big chain. Just a little one-site business. We thought long and hard about it because of the security issues, but we've done a good job of keeping the kids out of the public eye—the lady who owned the coffee shop didn't even know who we were—and so we let her take the job. It was expensive having a guy sit in the parking lot watching the place, but I was proud that she wanted to work. She thought it would be fun and I thought it would be a good experience."

"Was it?"

"As a matter of fact, it was. And she learned a great lesson from it, as well. For the first few weeks she was bringing home about twenty-five dollars a day in tips. But then all of a sudden her tips jumped significantly, up to nearly seventy-five dollars on many days. Obviously, I wanted to know what was going on. She said, 'I finally figured people out.' Well, I wanted to know what the new insight was. 'Dad,' she said, 'people *love* to talk about themselves! I used to just make their coffee and not say much. Now I ask them all kinds of questions about themselves.' That was it. By getting people to talk to her about their lives she was subconsciously influencing them to tip her more.

"She would ask them where they worked, how long they worked there, what kind of job they had, whether they liked it or not, how far they lived from work, whether they were married or had kids, things like that. All of this showed she was taking an interest in them as people. If you want to develop lasting relationships you have to be interesting. Nobody wants to hang out with a bore. But even more important than being interest*ing*, is being interest*ed*. That is a great lesson for leadership and influence in business. Do that, and you will always have influence and you will build any empire you like."

Marcus and Bobby continued on the tour of the stadium before going back up to see the last few innings. Bobby's team won, which made the event even more enjoyable. The next day Bobby and Marcus put work off and traveled to Bobby's lake house. Bobby's wife and kids joined them for the late afternoon and dinner, and Marcus got a firsthand look at what a family man his mentor was.

The next day the men got up early and played a round

of golf with two of Bobby's business associates. They didn't talk any business. Marcus wondered when they would get to the next lesson. He had enjoyed the first three and could see how well they complemented what he had learned in business school.

Early in the afternoon Bobby announced that they would be going back to New York that evening to prepare for a meeting the next day.

"What do you have planned for us there?"

"Trivia question. I am number ten on the list of wealthiest Americans. Who is number nine?"

"Gee, I have no idea."

"Paul Diamond."

"We're meeting Paul Diamond?"

"We are."

"Man, who would have imagined this? A kid from middle America spending the day with two of the richest guys in the world, whose names are Gold and Diamond. Diamond can't possibly be his real name, can it?"

"I think it is. Gold is my real name."

"I can see Gold, but come on, *Diamond?* It has to be a branding ploy."

"No, I think that is his real name. Pretty fortuitous though—just like my last name. Whenever I tell him that

Nothing's Better Than Gold, he likes to remind me that while he may not be better, he *is* richer. Not for long, though!"

Soon they were aloft again, on their way back to the Big Apple, to give Marcus the opportunity to meet none other than the biggest billionaire brand in the world: Paul Diamond.

GOLDEN RULE OF INFLUENCE NUMBER FOUR: DON'T SETTLE FOR ANYTHING LESS THAN EXCELLENCE

Paul Diamond's name was synonymous with excellence. No other human on earth had built a personal brand more recognizable. It didn't hurt that his name was *Diamond*, but the kind of person he was, he would have been influential if his name had been Mudd. Diamond started out building homes and moved into big-time commercial real estate in New York City. In only two decades he came to be considered by most as the king of that market, which was no small feat considering that New York City is home to some of the greatest real estate entrepreneurs in the world.

These days Diamond's big on hotels—you'll find a Diamond Hotel in almost every major city in the world.

Paul and Bobby Gold had known each other for over twenty years, and while you wouldn't call them good friends, they were very good acquaintances and spoke regularly. They had a mutual respect for each other that ran deep.

Bobby certainly could teach Marcus the last Golden Rule himself but thought Marcus would get a kick out of meeting the legend of Paul Diamond. As the men climbed back into the Navigators, Bobby informed Marcus the meeting with Diamond would be held at, where else, the New York Diamond Hotel. Paul's large set of suites high in the hotel served as his home base. As they drove, Bobby prepped Marcus for the meeting.

"You'll enjoy meeting Paul. He is a great guy. He has built his entire life on principles similar to the Golden Rules. Especially the last one."

"Which is?" Marcus asked.

"Golden Rule of Influence Number Four: Don't settle for anything less than excellence."

"Sounds great. I can't wait."

As the SUVs pulled in, the men stepped out and were soon whisked up to Diamond's suites.

As Bobby made the introductions, Marcus couldn't help but notice the view. "Wow, incredible," he said.

"Nothing but the best," Paul said.

"That's sort of why we're here," Bobby said. "As I mentioned on the phone, Marcus just graduated from Northwestern's business school and now I'm showing him the ropes a little bit, introducing him to a few folks who can give him some insights. I thought you would be a great person to teach him the value of excellence. What I am trying to really impress upon him is the idea of influence. I know that you and I both believe that our commitment to excellence gives us a great ability to build the kinds of businesses and reputations that allow us to have the kind of influence that we have."

"Well, that is very kind of you, Bobby—to give me the opportunity to share a few things. You could have done a fantastic job of that yourself, but I'm glad to help. Let's sit down." Paul led Bobby and Marcus to a couch and chairs in front of a giant floor-to-ceiling window with views that made you feel like you were walking in the air.

"You know, Marcus," Paul began, "Bobby is right: There is a huge connection between excellence and influence. People are attracted to excellence, so when we live our lives with excellence, people view us in a different way than if we didn't. They actually respect us more, admire us more, and give us more opportunity to influence them. You see, there are really only three options on how to live your life: poor, good, and excellent. Sure, you might be better in some areas than others, but that's basically it. Now, I realized a long time ago, as did Bobby, that if you want to win at life, if you want to be a leader and influencer, you are best served by living a life of excellence. Frankly, as I mentioned before, people are attracted to excellence. Have you ever heard about this concept, the 'law of attraction'?"

"Sure, it seems like everyone is talking about it these days."

"Well, call me a simpleton—a very rich simpleton—but I don't seem to get why everyone is making it out to be such a deep concept. Here's what the law of attraction means to me: The way you live your life either attracts people or repels people. That's it. Success in business is built around dealing and working with people. You want people to want to do business with you. When they want to do business with you, you have influence. It is as simple as that. Life's pretty simple. It's hard too, but mostly simple.

"People are attracted to excellence because they want to have more and be more excellent themselves. That is why they have all these TV shows about the homes and lifestyles of successful people. When people see excellence, they want it. They are attracted to it. When they see a lack of excellence, they run.

"With that in mind, I wanted to attract as many people and as much business as I could into my life, so I have based my life and work around seven areas of excellence: physical appearance, emotional health, intellectual growth, spiritual depth, relationships, financial success, and charitable giving. My goal is to be constantly improving in every area of my life, first for my own well-being, but also because I know that if I improve myself, I grow my influence."

"Which is what I was teaching you about transformation and working on yourself," Bobby interjected.

Paul continued. "He's right. When I first started out, I wasn't the Paul Diamond that you see now in magazines and newspapers and on television. No, I was not anywhere near what I am now. Most people don't realize that. Every one of us starts out the same: about seven pounds, twenty-two inches, and naked. From there, our lives are governed by our choices. If we make excellent choices, then we achieve even more excellence. Success begets success, so to speak. Let me tell you a little bit about each one of the areas."

"Please do," Marcus responded.

"If what Bobby tells me is true, you have the skills, Marcus. You have the knowledge. What you become now will depend on holding yourself to these standards of excellence. So, let's talk about physical appearance."

"Yeah, Bobby talked to me about first impressions."

"Very good. There are two kinds of impressions: *first* impressions and *lasting* impressions. Both of those are based on excellence. Having high standards for how you dress, what kind of shape you are in, and how you groom yourself are all a very significant part of the impression you leave with others. This doesn't mean you have to have movie-star good looks—I certainly don't have them. It does mean that you do the best with what you have. And from the looks of it, it looks like you do."

"Glad I passed that test," Marcus said, laughing.

"All right, emotional health. You know, business is tough. Life is tough. Deals go bad, people get sick, things don't happen the way you want them to. The people who succeed and rise to the top are the people who can handle whatever life throws at them. If you want to have influence, you have to succeed in a tumultuous world. The bigger the business, the bigger the problems and obstacles. These things all produce challenges and stress. How you handle them determines the heights you will achieve and the influence you will gain. So I take very good care of myself emotionally. I actually see a counselor periodically just to talk through all my stuff."

Diamond could see the surprise on Marcus's face. "Taking care of yourself emotionally isn't a sign of weakness, Marcus. People who *won't* deal with their emotions show their weakness. And, taking care of your emotions is good business. I take lots of vacation time to recharge myself. I also give lots of vacation time to my employees so they can recharge—and I *forbid* them to touch their BlackBerries when they're on vacation."

"Doesn't that diminish productivity?" Marcus asked.

"No, I believe it *improves* productivity. I would rather have people at one hundred percent for forty-six weeks than seventy percent for fifty-one. Take care of your emotions. People are attracted to those who are emotionally strong.

"About the next: intellectual growth. Do you know how many people never even pick up a book? Too many. And a lot of folks only pick up romance or espionage novels. Those are fine every now and then for an escape, but, come on, you also have to read books that help you learn and grow. And guess what happens when you do?"

"What?"

"You become a leader. An influencer. You might think that since you are out of school you will not have to read. Yes, you will read business stuff, which is great, but also challenge yourself to read books that will help you to grow. Listen to audio programs that will challenge your thinking. I am very staunch in my political beliefs, but I read books by leaders from the other party. I want to learn. I want to grow. I want to stretch. You should, too. So keep hitting the books. The competition won't be, and you will see the difference."

"The next one is an important one, Marcus," Bobby interjected. "Paul and I have discussed this a number of times."

"Spiritual depth. Spirituality is a topic that gets a bad rap in the media, but the fact is that people of great spirituality have been leaders for millennia. I believe that people who are strong spiritually are attractive to others. Now, I don't mean dogmatic people. I don't mean people who beat others up with their Bibles. I do mean people who have asked these important questions and come to the answers and developed a strong peace about them. Spiritual depth is essential to influence and leadership, I think," Paul said.

"I have never really given it much thought before," Marcus said.

"That's the problem. Humans are spiritual people. Yet most people spend more time figuring out their insurance needs than they do their spiritual needs. We ought to excel in that area, as well. Don't forget that. If humans are spiritual people, then they are more likely to be influenced by people who excel in their spirituality."

"I'll remember."

"All right, number five: relationships. I know Bobby has probably talked about relationships with you, right, Bobby?"

"Yes, we have discussed that, but any insights you have would be great."

"Certainly business relationships are important, but there are two areas that I think many businesspeople neglect and it brings them to an imbalance in their lives, which works against their success and influence. I am talking about family and friends. Many people like to give off the appearance of being a family man, but when push comes to shove, they stay at work rather than go home for dinner. When you have a family, go home for dinner, Marcus. Sure, there will be times that you have to work long hours, but the reality is that the work will be there when you come back in the morning. Your family can love you back. Your work can't."

"Those are good words, but I don't have a family of my own yet, just friends."

"Ah, friends. One of the great tragedies of our society is that businesspeople, especially men, neglect their friendships. I can't tell you how many men I know who have no friends to share their lives with. Now, you are young and going to school. When things heat up and you get busy and start a family, be sure to spend time with your friends."

"You seem so busy. Do you do that?"

"Absolutely. I go on hunting trips, vacations, you name it. I have four friends that I spend a great deal of time with. And we bring our wives and families together as much as we can. Sometimes we talk business, but we mostly talk life. That makes me a stronger person. *And* a better businessperson. Keep that in mind." Paul looked at the clock. "I only have ten more minutes or so before the mayor comes by. Forgive me for not being able to chat longer.

"The last two go hand in hand: financial success and charitable giving. If you excel in both, you can have tremendous influence in the world around you. Want to know how it works?"

"I sure do."

"You can gain influence by making money and gain even more by giving it away. Coming and going. Pretty great, actually. The more money you have, the more successful you are, the more people look up to you and are attracted to you. I am not saying that makes it a good thing, it just is. In fact, I know so many people who don't make a lot of money who are influential in other ways. Firemen, police officers, ministers; there are lots of people who serve our country in low-paying jobs who make a tremendous impact on our society. What I am saying is that if you are going into business to make money, excel at it. Make as much as you can. Obviously, keep your integrity and treat people fairly, but if you also want financial success, aim high. You will see that as you do, people will seek out your thoughts and opinions."

"But it doesn't guarantee it, does it?"

"Good point. I know my share of rich people who lost their influence because they didn't hold themselves to the same standards of excellence in the other areas of their lives.

"Which brings me back to charity. There is an old saying, 'To whom much has been given, much shall be required.' I believe that. I have more money than I know what to do with. I could retire the next five generations of my family. Believe me, they will get a great head start in life with the millions of dollars in trusts I have established, but I am focusing most of my wealth on changing the world through organizations in developing countries."

"Really?"

"Sure, what does each of my kids need more than ten or twenty million for? The rest will be given away while I am alive and also put into charitable trusts that my descendants will run to help make the world a better place. There are millions of men and women with great potential who have the deck stacked against them simply because of where they live or because they were born into poverty. I want to do what I can to help them. And do you know what happens when I do?"

"You gain more influence."

"Bingo."

"Okay, but most people don't have twenty billion dollars to work with. What about someone like me?"

"Fair question. You do the best you can. The more you have, the more you give. I don't look down on someone who makes three thousand dollars a month who gives away three hundred of it. That is every bit as admirable as the billionaire who gives away millions. And if we could get everyone to excel in this way, the world would be a better place."

Paul got up and walked to his bookshelf and pulled off a book he had written about five years ago. "Have you read this?" he asked.

"No, I haven't," Marcus said sheepishly.

"Tsk tsk," Diamond said with a smile. He pulled out a pen and signed it. *To Marcus, Excellence! Paul Diamond.*

"One last thing, Marcus. Excellence is something we practice in even the smallest details. You know, when I am walking through one of my properties, if I see a small scrap of paper on the floor, I personally stop and pick it up. I don't go to the manager and have him or her get someone to do it. I do it myself. And do you know what happens?"

"What?"

"My staff sees that even the small details matter to me. They get it. They see that I lead by example. It inspires them to pay attention to even the smallest details too. Excellence in everything we do is what makes guys like Bobby and me so influential." Paul looked at his watch. "Well, I would love to chat more but I need a few minutes to get some paperwork together before the mayor gets here. Bobby, always a pleasure."

"Thanks, Paul, I owe you a round of golf for your time."

Paul looked at Marcus and laughingly said, "Sure, he

'repays' me by picking the one thing he is better at than me!"

"Thanks, Mr. Diamond," Marcus said.

"No problem. Always willing to help others excel. You do the same."

"I will."

NEW BEGINNINGS

Marcus was surprised to find out that Bobby wasn't going to be joining him for the flight home. "No, I have too much work here the next couple of days. Then back to Chicago. Ned will take good care of you though."

"Well, thank you so much, Bobby. You cannot even begin to imagine what a gift this has been. I hope we can keep in touch."

"Absolutely. You have my cell number. Call any time. You are a good kid. You remind me of myself at your age."

"Thanks, that is a great compliment."

"All right, I have to get going. Safe travels."

Marcus stepped on the plane and prepared for take-off. After about twenty minutes of flight he noticed a small box on one of the tables in the rear of the plane. Attached was a card with his name on it, so he opened it up. The first thing he noticed was a wall hanging inscribed with the Four Golden Rules of Influence:

LIVE A LIFE OF UNDIVIDED INTEGRITY

ALWAYS DEMONSTRATE A POSITIVE ATTITUDE

CONSIDER OTHER PEOPLE'S INTERESTS AS
MORE IMPORTANT THAN YOUR OWN

DON'T SETTLE FOR ANYTHING LESS
THAN EXCELLENCE

Inside the box was another card, which read:

Marcus, it was great meeting you. I think you're a terrific young man who is destined for good things. And I *am glad to have found out what happened to my favorite nanny. Be sure to tell her hello for me. She had a significant impact on me as a child during a rough time. Which brings me to the point of this note: I have always wanted to repay your grandmother. That's what this weekend was about. But there is a little twist. Your brother Jack has a lot of gumption—good gumption—and he loves you and believes in you. He took the liberty of faxing me a copy of that business plan you've been working so hard on. Looks very interesting and I think it has some legs to it. So, consider this check a gift to get it started. If you like, I will serve as an adviser, as well. If you get your business up and running with the gift I am giving you, I will be willing to invest $500,000 in exchange for a forty percent stake in the business. My only other requirement is that when you hit it big, you have to use your wealth and influence to help others. I look forward to getting to know you better. Your new friend in influence, Bobby Gold.*

As Marcus looked in the box, his brother's words came back to him, "Don't mess this up." So that's what he meant. Jack was looking for an investor for Marcus's new business.

It was time to see what kind of gift Bobby had given him. He looked at the check: $50,000 written from a personal account. "Wow," Marcus said out loud. He turned and looked out the window at the horizon. He couldn't believe what had happened in the last few weeks. He decided then and there to make Bobby proud of his investment.

Thirty minutes later the phone rang. Marcus didn't know whether to answer it but finally did because it kept ringing.

"I was hoping you would answer," came Bobby's voice. "Did you open your present?"

"I did. That is amazing, Bobby. I don't know what to say or do."

"Do your best. Make a difference. We need all the influencers we can get to make the most of this world. Just give it your best."

"I will, Bobby. I promise."

"Very good. I gotta run. Let's talk in a few weeks."

They hung up. Marcus thought to himself, *Nothing's Better Than Gold*, then returned his gaze to the horizon. The entire world was before him. He was determined to influence it in the most significant way he could.

ACKNOWLEDGMENTS

I would like to acknowledge a number of people. First, the great team at Chris Widener International. You are fantastic!

Second, my agents at the absolutely terrific DSM Agency: Doris Michaels, Delia Berrigan-Fakis, and the rest of the team there.

Third, my editors, Sarah Rainone and Roger Scholl. Thanks for your dedication to making *The Art of Influence* the best book it could be.

Fourth, a few others who have spoken and written on influence as well: Robert Cialdini, the author of *Influence:*

The Psychology of Persuasion; Kurt Mortensen, author of *Maximum Influence: The 12 Universal Laws of Power Persuasion;* and Debra Pestrak, a fellow National Speakers Association member and owner of www.ArtOfInfluence.com. Each of these people has contributed to the discussion of positive influence in a tremendous way.

Fifth, the close friends who influence me: Dino, Bryan, Kevin, and Jeff. Thanks for your friendship.

Most importantly, my wife and children: Lisa, Christopher, Hannah, Rebekah, and Sarah—my partners in influencing the world and making a difference.

ABOUT THE AUTHOR

Chris Widener is a successful businessman, author, speaker, and television host.

He has authored over 450 articles and 9 books, including a *New York Times* and *Wall Street Journal* bestseller. He has produced over 85 CDs and DVDs on leadership, motivation, and success.

Chris is the host of *Made for Success* and co-host of *True Performance* with Zig Ziglar. Chris is also a featured columnist for *Success* magazine.

The Chris Widener newsletter, *Made for Success*, is one of the most widely distributed newsletters on personal and professional development. Personal-development legends such as Zig Ziglar, John Maxwell, Brian Tracy, Jim Rohn, and Denis Waitley have lauded Chris's work, and many consider him the leader of a new generation of personal-development experts.

CHRIS WIDENER RESOURCES

ACHIEVE A HIGHER
LEVEL OF SUCCESS

Now that you've enjoyed *The Art of Influence*, explore Chris Widener's other exceptional works that provide life-changing principles of leadership, motivation, and success.

MADE FOR SUCCESS SERIES

 Chris learned early on that if you're interested in achieving success faster and with fewer struggles, then one of the easiest ways is to learn how other successful people did it and simply . . . copy them!

This incredible DVD/CD set features in-depth interviews with 23 of today's most renowned experts in their fields, including America's foremost business philosopher Jim Rohn, bestselling coauthor of the *Chicken Soup for the Soul* series Mark Victor Hansen, San Antonio Spurs mental training coach David Cook, former NFL quarterback Tom Flick, former CFO of Microsoft John Connors, and many more.
23 DVDs/CDs

THE EXTRAORDINARY LEADERS SEMINAR

Make yourself into an extraordinary leader! Learn the character traits and skills of leaders, the ways to develop leaders, leadership myths and mistakes, and more!

13 CDs with downloadable workbook

THE ULTIMATE SUCCESS SERIES

Chris's definitive discussions on a variety of success and leadership principles. This important series includes The Ultimate Time Management Seminar, Bringing Balance to a Chaotic Life, Live the Life You Have Always Dreamed Of, The "Best" Test, Right Now Leadership—What You Can Do to Be a Better Leader, Finding Financial Freedom to Ensure a Fantastic Financial Finish, and Seven Minutes to Success.

12 CDs

CHRIS WIDENER CAN MOTIVATE AND INSPIRE YOUR TEAM IN PERSON!

For years, audiences have enjoyed Chris Widener's engaging and versatile speaking style and his ability to educate and train while instilling humor, excitement, and passion. For your next event or meeting, consider booking Chris for the very best lectures or seminars on inspiration, leadership, success, and personal development. His topics include:

- Twelve Pillars of Success
- Winning with Influence
- Leadership Rules of Engagement:
  Creating Fully Engaged Followers
- Leading Your Organization Through Change
- Secrets of Motivating Others to Follow Your Leadership
- Right Now Leadership: What You Can Do Today
  to Become a Better Leader
- Live the Life You Have Always Dreamed Of!
- Dare to Dream

For more information or to reserve an engagement, e-mail Chris's exclusive booking agent at speaker@yoursuccessstore. com or call 877-929-0439.